A Few Remarks In Reply To Mr. Pinkerton: Upon The Scarcity Of Men Of Genius At Naples

Joseph Binnie

In the interest of creating a more extensive selection of rare historical book reprints, we have chosen to reproduce this title even though it may possibly have occasional imperfections such as missing and blurred pages, missing text, poor pictures, markings, dark backgrounds and other reproduction issues beyond our control. Because this work is culturally important, we have made it available as a part of our commitment to protecting, preserving and promoting the world's literature. Thank you for your understanding.

A FEW

REMARKS

IN REPLY TO

MR. PINKERTON,

UPON

The Scarcity of Men of Genius at Naples, in recent times,

AS ASSERTED IN HIS

"MODERN GEOGRAPHY."

BY

A NEAPOLITAN.

Bristol:

PRINTED BY JOHN EVANS, AT THE MERCURY-OFFICE,
34, BROAD-STREET.

1810.

ERRATA.

In page 24, line 2, for St. Giovannina Carbonara, *read* St. Giovanni a Carbonara ; and in line 5, for Study, *read* Studj.

In page 27, in note, line 2, for advisers, *read* advices.

In the second page of note at the end marked †, line 22, for replied, *read* repeated, and in line 31, for peat, *read* pent.

In the sixth page of third note, marked ‡, line 12, *read* Academics, Peripatetics, and Stoics.

REMARKS.

IN the second volume, page 639, of Mr. PINKERTON's work of Modern Geography, are these words:

"Few men of distinguished genius have re-
"cently appeared in this portion of Italy,"
(meaning the kingdom of Naples,) "which is
"over-run with priests and lawyers; but among
"the latter, *Giannone* has distinguished himself
"by his spirited history of his country."

Naturally desirous that my country should hold her proper rank in the commonwealth of letters, I wish to correct this mistake of the author of Modern Geography. Instead of saying, "Few men of distinguished genius have "recently appeared in this portion of Italy," he should, for truth's sake, have better said,— *that a great many distinguished geniuses have always flourished in this portion of Italy, not excepting modern or recent times.* Had Mr. Pinkerton taken the trouble to enquire, he must have been instructed from books and verbal information, that the following great men were all of the kingdom of Naples, not including Sicily. And it being the principal object of this tract to prove the solidity of the latter assertion, I shall submit to the reader a general progressive statement of them all, at all times.

ANCIENTS.

Livius Andronicus,[1] *Gneus Nevius,*[2] *Ennius,*[3] *Cajus Lucilius,*[4] *C. Marius, Cicero,*[5] *Ovid,*[6] *Statius,*[7] *Juvenal,*[8] *Horace,*[9] *Vitruvius,*[10] *Numisius,*[11] *C. V. Paterculus,*[12] *&c.*

[1] Tiraboschi thinks him a native of Magna Græcia, in Calabria. He was the father of dramatic poetry at Rome.

[2] He was of Campania, and a very correct writer of dramatic works. Cicero, de Oratore, thinks that Nevius and Plautus were the patterns of Latin purity.

[3] He was of Rudia, in the province of Lecce. The merit of his heroic works is well known.

[4] He was a native of Sessa, in Campania, mentioned by Juvenal, in Sat. I. author of celebrated Satires.

[5] Of Arpino.

[6] A native of Sulmona, in Abruzzo, of an illustrious family.

[7] He was of the city of Naples, and lived under Domitian, of whom he had been preceptor. We have by him two celebrated poems, the Thebaide, and the Achilleide.

[8] This famous Satirist of the first century of our æra, was born in Aquino.

[9] Every body knows that Venosa had the honor to be the native country of this great poet, who lived in the century of Augustus, and was born in the 36th year before Christ.

[10] By a great many antiquarians, Vitruvius is considered a Neapolitan of Campania; though it is the opinion of some that he was of Verona.

[11] Numidius, or Numisius, was another famous architect, and lived with Vitruvius. He was the constructor of the famous Theatre of Herculaneum, and is believed to be a native of Campania.

[12] He was born at Naples; his name was Cajus Vellejus Paterculus, a famous historian. We have of him the Vellejan Annals; in Italian, Annali Vellejani.

IN TIMES OF DARKNESS AND BARBARISM.

The famous *Cassiodoro*, one of the few luminaries of his times; who was the guide of the barbarian Theodorick, and succeeded in making of him a good and magnanimous prince.

NEARER TO US, OR FROM THE TWELFTH CENTURY DOWNWARD.

St. Thomas d'Aquino, the most celebrated doctor in divinity that ever existed.

Flavius Gioja, discoverer of the maritime compass.

Andrew d'Isernia, a man of great note in the law.

Jovian Pontano, philosopher, poet, orator, and a classical scholar, at the head of the famous Ancient Academy of Sciences and Literature at Naples, which existed since the epoch of the great Alphonso the First, under the direction of *Anthony Beccadelli, Bartolomew Fazio,* and *Laurence Valla,* men of distinguished note.

The learned English author of the Life of Leo the Tenth, has honored the memory of Pontano with the following mention: " Few scholars " who have owed their eminence merely to their

"talents, have enjoyed a degree of respect and
"dignity equal to Pontano."—Vol. 1. cap. xi.
page 88.

Junianus Majo, an illustrious grammarian, instructor of *James Sannazzaro,* who was a poet of the first class, and author of the celebrated Arcadia, and several other classical works.

The famous *Cariteo,* another eminent poet, with many other fellow-scholars, viz. *Acquaviva, Alessandri, Cavaniglia, Carbone, Poderico,* &c.

The famous *Pomponius Leto,* a classical scholar and eminent orator.

Serafinus d'Aquila, eminent likewise for his literature and poetry.

Simon and *Camillus Porzio,* father and son, the first the greatest philosopher of his time; the second a good historian.

Camillus Pellegrini, author of the Antiqua Capua, a very learned historian.

Angelus di Costanzo, an eminent historian and poet; with many others after him, viz. Cardinal *Baronio, John Villano, Thomas Costo, Cesar Capaccio, Anthony Summonte, Francis Capocelatro,* and the famous *Scipio Ammirato*, author of the celebrated History of Florence, and several other works.

Bernardinus Telesio, the most respected philosopher of his time.

Giordanus Bruno,[1] the precursor of the enlightened philosophy.

Marcus Aurelius Severino, celebrated doctor in physic.

John Baptist della Porta,[2] very well known as a great mathematician and natural philosopher, and for the number of his works upon various subjects. He was the founder of a very select Academy of Sciences at his own house.

[1] He lived in the time of Queen Elizabeth, and was a native of Nola, a few miles from Naples. He dared to write, against the prejudices and superstitions of his time, his famous book, Spaccio Della Bestia Trionfante, obliged him to leave the continent for England. He was received at that court, and became acquainted with Sidney and Grenville, two famous characters of those times. But returning to Venice, he was arrested by the Inquisition, and burned alive.

[2] Porta was the inventor of the combination of two lenses in telescopes, before Galilei. He was a native of the city of Naples, of a respectable family, and died in the year 1515.

Bernardinus Rota, an excellent poet.

Aloisius Lilio, the author of the present form of the Gregorian calendar.

Bartolomew Eustachio, a celebrated discoverer in anatomy. His anatomical tables are considered a master-piece in that science.

Fabius Colonna, a great botanist and discoverer of the plant valeriana columna.[1]

Torquatus Tasso, who needs no comment upon his celebrity.

And the two following ilustrious women for poetry, *Vittoria Colonna*,[2] and *Tullia d'Aragona*.

---

[1] This classical naturalist was born in the year 1567, and died in 1647. At the age of 24, he published his famous Fitobasano, in which he describes several plants known to the ancients, and demonstrates that the ancient names of them correspond with the modern. He not only discovered the plant valeriana, so useful in diseases of the nerves, but was the inventor of the system distinguishing the differences of plants from their seeds and fruits, which system was imitated by Tournefort. Dr. Bianchi has written the Life of this great man.

[2] She married Ferdinand Avalos, Marquis of Pescara, a gallant officer of the Emperor Charles V. and was celebrated for her beauty, genius, and virtues. Her poetical works were published at Naples, in 8vo. 1548.

John Alfonce Borelli, one of the greatest professors of philosophy and mathematics.

Francis Fontana, astronomer.

Chevalier d'Arpino,[1] a celebrated painter, with *Santafede,*[2] *Massimo,*[3] *Spagnoletto,*[4] *Vaccaro,*[5]

[1] His name was Joseph Cesare, native of Arpino, the country of Cicero and Marius. He went to France with the Cardinal Aldobrandini, where he was decorated by the King with the Cross of St. Michael. He was one of the twelve best painters selected by Philip III. King of Spain, to represent the most remarkable events of the Roman history.

[2] Fabrizio Santafede, of Naples, was born in 1560. Though not considered a painter of the first class, yet from the excellence of his portraits, he was called the Neapolitan Apelles. The people held his works in so much respect, that when in the revolution of 1647, the mob were about to burn the house of a Nicholas Balsamo, one cried, "*Stop! there are the pictures of Santafede;*" and the attempt was declined.

[3] Chevalier Massimo Stanzioni was his name. He was born at Naples in 1585. He studied after Caracci and Guido very much, and succeeded in adopting the taste of the former, and the stile of the latter. He was created Knight by the Pope Urbano VIII. as a reward for two famous pictures made by him at Rome, of the Marriage and Martyrdom of St. Catharina.

[4] Joseph Ribera was born in Gallipoli, of the province of Lecce, in the year 1593, called Spagnoletto, because his father was a Spanish officer. Michelangelo da Caravaggio was his master, but he went to Rome and Parma to study Raffael and Correggio. He made a large fortune, and lived in a very luxurious stile. The Viceroy of Naples, then

8.

Falcone,[1] *Micco Spataro,*[2] *Calabrese,*[3] *Salvator*

Don Giovanni d'Austria, having seduced his eldest daughter, and taken her away from home, the father, seized with a deep melancholy, left his house, and was never more seen.

[3] This painter was of the city of Naples, born in the year 1670. His master was Caravaggio, but following the advice of his friend Massimo, he improved his manner upon the noble stile of Guido. The Judgment of Solomon is one of his master-pieces, and in possession of the Count of Harac, at Vienna.

[1] Aniello Falcone, of Naples, may be considered a classical painter of battles. He has been indeed, the wonder of his profession. It is said, that Bourgognone, so much renowned likewise for battle-pieces, went to see this famous Neapolitan, and asked two of his battles in exchange for two of his own. Falcone was excellent in drawing, and the best imitator of nature. He had several good scholars, among the most distinguished was Domenico Gargiulo, called [2] Micco Spataro, (perhaps from his bravery in fencing, in which also he was excellent,) who left to posterity from his wonderful pencil, the living memory of the most remarkable events of his times,—the dreadful conflagrations of Mount Vesuvius, the awful calamity of the plague, and several insurrections of the people, painted with liveliness, truth, and intelligence. Indeed, nothing interests more the human understanding at large, than the sight of those events so masterly represented.

[3] His name was Chevalier Mattia Preti, born on the 24th of February 1613, in Traverna of Calabria, and thence called Calabrese. He travelled a great deal through Italy, France, and Flanders, for the purpose of improvement. This noble artist is remarked for his excellent outlines, and for the strength of his pencil. His best productions are to be seen at Naples and Rome, but he painted in several other parts of Europe.

Rosa,[1] *de Matteis, Giordano,* and many others.

John da Nola, a sculptor of great note, with *Santa Croce, Cosimo, d'Auria,* and *Laurent Vaccaro.*

Masuccio the second, distinguished architect, restorer of the Grecian architecture. He perfected the Ionick order.

And *Chevalier Bernini,* likewise a famous architect and sculptor.

Chevalier Marini, author of the two celebrated poems, the Adone, and the Massacre of the Innocents.

[1] Salvator Rosa is really the honour of the Neapolitan pencil. He was born at Naples, in the year 1615, and was fellow-scholar with Micco Spataro, under Aniello Falcone. He is celebrated for his landscapes, and was also a man of learning, a poet, and a great heroical painter. The author of this note being one morning with a lady, in Rome, observing the famous Dorian gallery, when they came to look at a picture of Salvator Rosa, the Death of Abel, which was in one of the back-rooms, the keeper presented a chair to the lady, saying, *" Here you must sit down Madam: I am sure this picture would keep you standing too long;"* and it was really so. After having inspected so many master-pieces, Salvator Rosa triumphed over all, creating in their minds a kind of fresh interest for astonishment and admiration. The keeper observed, *" He was obliged to keep chairs in that part of the gallery, because at no other picture were people used to remain standing so long."*

The respectable number of distinguished men of genius already mentioned, who flourished after the twelfth century, or from the revival of letters downward, must be taken as forming subjects of modern history; for its period is fixed to that of *Charlemagne*, that is, from the eighth century of our æra. I do not see why they ought not to be considered also as forming subjects of modern geography. Who ever separated geography from history? They have been considered always as two sisters, one sitting upon the lap of the other. I wonder then that Mr. Pinkerton, after having given the title of modern geography to his work, in mentioning the writers of this period, descends so low as to the beginning of the last century, when *Giannone* lived: and his expression of "few" cannot be reconciled with the large number of those men of learning and genius who preceded *Giannone*, as we have already demonstrated, nor with those who lived with and after him, as we are about to prove.

MEN OF GENIUS WITH AND AFTER *GIANNONE* TILL VERY NEAR TO US.

Francis d'Andrea[1] and *Dominicus d'Aulisio*, two learned and famous lawyers and orators.

---

[1] This great man was born on the 24th of February, 1625, in a little town called Ravello, on the coast of Amalfi. Indeed, he was the most learned lawyer and orator of all Europe.

John Vincent Gravina, the greatest scholar in the world, author of several admired works, and

At Naples, they called him the second Neapolitan Cicero. He defended the right of his Sovereign Charles II. King of Spain, to the dukedom of Brabante, against the King of France; and although a great many learned people throughout all Europe wrote upon the subject, Andrea's works only were crowned with laurels. Such was his repute, that in a journey through Italy, he was obliged very often to make a speech extempore, to satisfy the wishes of the people to hear his elocution. He expelled the barbarism introduced at the bar in that time, and promoted the purity and the true spirit of the law. He left to posterity several works, which are mentioned by Tiraboschi. After a glorious career, he retired to Candela, a little village near Melfi, where he closed his days on the 10th of September, 1698. Not less conspicuous were the two following, Aulisio and Gravina, not only in the science of the laws, but in any other branch of learning. Aulisio was the preceptor of Giannone in the law, and the author of a great many valuable works, viz. Raggionamenti intorno a principj della Filosofia e Teologia degli Assirii, e dell' Arte d'Indovinare de' stessi popoli.—La Poesia Fenicia.—De Ortu et Progressu Medicinæ, &c. He was of the city of Naples, born in the year 1649, and died in 1717. The other great genius, Gravina, was of Regio, near Cosenza, in Calabria, born on the 21st of January, 1664. He studied with Aulisio, and became so profound in literature, that he was considered the most learned man of the beginning of the last century. He lived a long while at Rome, where he was not only professor of law in the University, but had the honor of laying the foundation of the poetical academy of Arcadia. Besides his capital work on the Origin of Laws, he wrote several tragedies, orations, poetry, and the two famous books, La Ragion Poetica. He died at Rome on the 6th of January 1718.

chiefly that of the Origin and Progress of Civil Laws.

George Baglivi, reckoned the best physician of Italy, of the last century.

Jacinto di Cristofaro,[1] an illustrious mathematician.

Nicholas Cirillo, the famous commentator of Aldrovandus, and president of the Academy of Sciences at Naples.

Nicolas Capasso, one of the greatest professors of the University in the law, and an eminent poet. He was likewise a classical orator.

[2] The famous masters of music, *Leo*, the two *Scarlattis*, *Alexander Porpora*, *Vinci*, *Feo*,

---

[1] He was born at Naples in 1650, and was the author of the treatise De Constructione Æquationum, published in 1700, and of the other work, Della Dottrina de Triangoli. On that occasion, he received a letter from the Academy of Sciences at Paris, of the date of July 6, 1701, in which were these words: "Vous nous faites bien voir, Monsieur, de quoi sont capable les Italiens."

[2] Among the many classical institutions peculiar to the Neapolitan school of music, the following, which was first introduced by Alexander Scarlatti, Leo, Greco, and Durante, and continued since them by Sala and Fenaroli, is worthy of notice, viz. that every young student should learn that part of vocal music called in Italian solfeggio, and the

Greco, Durante, who was the father of the best Neapolitan school of music.

fundamental rules of the science at large, before he undertook the practice of any kind of instrument. Two useful consequences arise from this institution—first, that all the instrumental performers are used to play, even the most difficult music, at sight; and in the second place, the knowledge of the general principles of the science enables a young man to determine for himself on that particular branch of it which is the best adapted to his genius. To this system we owe the divine compositions of Pergolese, who feeling his genius soar above mere execution, abandoned the violin, to the practice of which he was originally destined, and evinced his taste for harmony by his compositions.— Another anecdote (which I had from an old professor at Naples) may serve to illustrate the same principle. When Handel was at Naples, his wonderful execution on the harpsichord excited the jealousy of all the Neapolitan professors. One night at a musical party he was particularly admired for his execution of a very difficult concerto. On looking around after the conclusion of it, Handel perceived Domenico Scarlatti (who though not twenty years of age, was in high repute for his performances) standing with his arms folded at the back of the room, and begged of him to sit down in his turn at the harpsichord and favour the company with a specimen of his abilities. The young man readily took the same concerto which was so masterly performed by Handel, and placing it, as if by mistake, the wrong way on the desk, performed to the admiration of the whole company, at first sight and upside-down, that very difficult concerto which Handel himself had composed or previously studied. I cannot trace any other authority for this anecdote, except what I received in a verbal communication. But this extraordinary man was celebrated for several other instances of his wonderful abilities. Something

And *Pergolese*, whose genius soared, perhaps, too high, escaped the reach of Mr. Pinkerton's sight.

The two great vocal performers, *Farinelli* and *Caffarelli*, men of honorable memory.

Anthony Genovese, a very good scholar, great speaker, and an eminent metaphysician, author of an excellent Institution on Commerce.

Joseph Aurelius de Gennaro, a great lawyer.

Scipion d'Afflitto, Canonico Mazzocchi, and *James Martorelli,* Grecians and antiquarians of

---

like it happened at Venice, when he confounded the famous Rosingrave, who gave to us authority for the fact in a letter written to Dr. Burney. In the same modest manner he was standing in a corner of the room of a musical party, when Rosingrave performed one of his best toccate, and with his very best success. But when the young Scarlatti afterwards sat at the harpsichord to play an extempore sonata, Rosingrave himself said, that "*He thought*" (these are the words of Dr. Burney in his work, the History of Music, vol. iv. page 26) "*ten hundred devils had been at the instrument; that he never had heard such passages of execution and effect before; that the performance so far surpassed his own, and every degree of perfection to which he thought it possible he should ever arrive, that if he had been in sight of any instrument with which to have done the deed, he should have cut off his own fingers.*" Rosingrave declared, "*He did not touch an instrument himself for a month after this rencontre.*"

eminent note. The latter was author of a very interesting work, the Grecian Colonies, and the Regia Thecacalamaria; and *Mazzocchi* has been considered the most learned man of Europe.

Charles Pecchia, an historian, author of the Civil and Political History of the Kingdom of Naples, a classical work very much admired throughout Europe.

Francis Grimaldi, author of the learned work, Annals of the Kingdom of Naples.

John Baptist Vico, a famous orator and philosopher, author of the celebrated work, La Scienza Nuova. He had two famous pupils, the Father *Ignazio della Croce*, and the Father *Gherardo de Angelis*, two sacred orators, in great estimation, throughout Italy. They have left capital works on literature, divinity, and sacred elocution.

The Bishop *Antinori*, a very learned man in antient history. He wrote the History of Abruzzo, whose fragments are inserted in the Annals of Muratori.

And *Paolo Moccia* and *Marco Mondo*, are two esteemed geniuses in Greek and Latin literature.

In these recent times, and towards the middle of the last century, flourished several very good dramatic writers, among whom was the Marquis *Liveri*, who distinguished himself by his comedies.

Unless Mr. Pinkerton is of opinion that men of genius at Naples ought to grow like potatoes in England, he should be satisfied with the honorable list of them already submitted to his review; and they are, according to his wishes, so recent, that I can recollect personally the greatest part of them all. But we now proceed to the rear, or rather to the still younger class of Neapolitan worthies.

FURTHER ACCOUNT OF MEN OF GENIUS WHO FLOURISHED TOWARDS THE LATTER END OF THE LAST CENTURY.

Father *della Torre*, naturalist, and discoverer of a wonderful microscope of an immense magnifying power.

Francis Serrao, the most celebrated doctor in physic of Naples, and a great naturalist. We have by him the best account of the Vesuvian eruptions.

Bartolomew Intieri, a very useful genius, discoverer of a machine for drying corn and preserving it from corruption for many years—a very valuable invention, carefully imitated in France and in Switzerland. The learned Duhamel, at Paris, has published a work upon this very invention: *vide* La Lande's Travels through Italy, vol. vii. page 293.

Bernard Galiani, the best illustrator of Vitruvius; and his brother the Abbé *Galiani*, a singular man for his wit. He was the most accomplished and agreeable man in company. He was an author at the age of 18. His works upon the Economy of Grain, and upon the Value of Coins, are very much esteemed.

Pascal Carcani, a distinguished antiquarian, at the head of the work on the Antiquities of Herculaneum.

Nicholas and *Peter de Martino*, and *Felix Sabatelli*, great professors of mathematics and astronomy.

Gaetano Flangieri, author of the celebrated work, La Filosofia della Giurisprudenza.

Marquis *Palmieri*, author of the known book, L'Arte della Guerra.

Joseph Pascal Cirillo, a great speaker and lawyer, one of the best professors of the

Neapolitan University, and author of the Codex Carolinus; the most learned man of Europe.

Joseph Sorge, Andrew Vignes, and *Charles Franchi,* all eminent lawyers and orators.

The illustrious woman *Signora Ardinghelli,* distinguished by her talents in physic. She is very well known in the republic of letters.

Nicholas Gnarra, a great antiquarian.

Father *Martini,* author of a classical work, the History of Music.

The famous *Jommelli, Sala,* and *Corelli;* the famous *Sacchini, Majo, Cafaro, Piccini, Cimarosa, Guiglielmi,* and *Sabatini,* all great geniuses, and as such esteemed by every one excepting Mr. Pinkerton.

Domenico Cirillo, an eminent physician, known by all the English of note who have been at Naples; one of the best botanists of our times. *Salvator Conforti,* a distinguished professor of divinity. *Marius Pagano,* author of the celebrated work, Processo Criminale, the Criminal Trial. *Pascal Baffi,* a classical professor of the Greek and Oriental languages.

Vito Caravelli, author of a very complete and general course of mathematics, and a professor of great note.

AND THE FOLLOWING ARE SUPPOSED TO BE STILL LIVING.

Father *Bertola,* famous for his genius of extempore poesy, author of several admired poetical compositions, and learned in languages, especially of the German, on which he has published the work, Idea della Poesia Alemanna, an Idea of the German Poetry.

Emanuel Campolongo, a very respected scholar, eminent professor of Rhetoric and Belles Letters in the University, author of the Mergellina, and several other admired poems.

Duca Belforte, reckoned the best poet of Italy. His work, Omaggio Poetico, on occasion of the marriage of the King, has been praised very much in the French journals; and his genius excels in the stiles of Anacreon and Pindar: see La Lande, in his Travels through Italy, vol. vii. page 241.

Cappelli and *Mattei* are likewise two very good poets. *Mattei* is the author of the work, Saggio di Poesie Italiane e Latine, and several others. His fine translation of the Miserere was set to music by Jommelli.

There are at Naples many geniuses admirable for extempore poesy; and besides, the before-mentioned *Bertola*, Messrs. *Mollo, Serio, Carta,* and *Massari,* are all people of astonishing ability, who will upon any given argument whatsoever, pronounce extempore a fine and learned dissertation in poetry. *Serio* is also a professor in the University of Italian elocution.

Who has not heard of *Paisiello?*

Raffael Morghen, the first engraver in the world.

Domenico Cotugno,[1] a physician of great note, and classical discoverer in anatomy.

---

[1] He is the discoverer of some little tubes in the ear, called by his name, Cotumnian's tubes. When they were discovered, it is said, that the famous Morgagni mentioned the case to his scholars in one of his public lectures, in the University of Padua, saying, that a wonderful Neapolitan young man, called Cotugno, had made such an important discovery. It happened by chance, that the very discoverer was among the audience, just come incognito from Naples, for the pleasure of hearing Morgagni; and at the end of the lecture he introduced himself to Morgagni, addressing him with the following words: "My master, if the sight of the person so much honored by your notice to-day, can afford to your great mind any additional interest, know, that he who now kisses your hand is Cotugno."

Here I must humbly beseech Mr. Pinkerton to shew me in his Modern Geography, in what part of the world I could find now living three other geniuses to be compared with those mentioned above. I am not able to discover even in England a *Paisiello*, a *Morghen*, or a *Cotugno*.[1]

Andreozzi, Amiconi, Curcio, Anfossi, Tritta, Marinelli, Monti, Zincarelli, are all great masters of music, now living.

Troja, a famous oculist, and author of many esteemed dissertations.

Philip Caulini, who has made many discoveries in natural history.

Cyrus Minervini, an able naturalist and antiquarian. He has published several works very well known.

---

[1] It is to be observed, that the writer's purpose is confined to the kingdom of Naples, for if he were to speak of all Italy, he could mention several other distinguished geniuses, perhaps, now living, that could with equal difficulty be rivalled any where else in the world, as Spallanzani, Canova, Alfieri, Cesarotti, &c. True it is, that the present learning may not be considered so classical as it was formerly in different periods; but this is now the general fate of Europe, and Naples stands in good proportion with any other country, notwithstanding its very small compass, being only a corner of Italy, and labouring under a great many obstacles and political obstructions to the improvement of talents.

Peter Signorelli, author of the learned work, Storia Critica de Teatri, and Vicende della Coltura delle due Sicilie.

The *Arvocato Galanti*, an interesting author, and patriotic writer upon the real interests of the kingdom of Naples and Sicily.

Secondo, Moccia, Grimaldi, Delfico, Poli, Andria, Fergola, and many others, now living, all authors of esteemed works on different branches of learning.

And I beg pardon, if I have neglected any other deserving notice and praise, whom my want of recollection or intelligence has overlooked, as I write entirely from memory.

The author of the said work, Modern Geography, says afterward, that the Neapolitan government is quite despotical; but he has neglected to mention a truth which may be entitled to more liberal notice,—that since the beginning of the thirteenth century, under the protection of the Great Frederick II. and his Mæcenas, the illustrious *Peter delle Vigne*, Neapolitan literature was revived and flourished in the two afterwards esteemed Universities, one at Salerno, (founded under the name of School[1] long before the

---

[1] We have from this very school the famous ancient book, Medicina Salernitana, dedicated to a King of England.

epoch of the Great Frederick,) and another in the city of Naples, which have existed ever since, notwithstanding the various disturbances, revolutions, and calamities of the country. And from these very Universities, as well as from many private and public academies of learning, and especially from that of the celebrated *Pontano*, immense numbers of very well informed people have issued.

A Neapolitan Academy of Sciences and Literature, recently under the patronage of Charles III. of Spain, then King of Naples, supplied men of great learning to illustrate the very interesting antiquities found in the ancient towns of Herculaneum and Pompei; in consequence of which was published the famous work upon this subject, which now forms a part of all the best libraries of Europe. I shall not neglect to mention again the learned *Carcani*, who chiefly was employed in this capital work.

Naples was finally decorated again[1] with a Royal Academy of Sciences and Belles Letters, in 1779.

There are also several public libraries, four of which are classical, one at St. Angelo a Nido;

[1] The first institution of the Royal Academy was under the reign of the Emperor Charles VI. until three years after the succession of Charles III. of Spain.

another in the convent of St. Domenico Maggiore; another at St. Giovanina Carbonara, with many valuable manuscripts; and the fourth, the most stupendous and complete, is in the royal building called Study; this magnificent building is the celebrated work of Chevalier *Fontana*. It was destined formerly for the University, but now, the University being removed, this very building has been much improved and enlarged. And there now exist not only the said Library, but the Academy of Painting, where youth (as well as in any other public institution) may receive education without any expence whatsoever. But there will be also a Botanical Garden, and a general grand Museum of all sorts of curiosities and master-pieces of fine arts, which now are to be seen partly at Portici, in the Royal Museum, where is admired a beautiful and large collection of all the ancient curiosities found in Herculaneum and Pompei; and especially the collection of bronzes, and ancient pictures in a kind of fresco, is one of the most singular in Europe. And partly at Capo di Monte, in the great palace of the King, where is exhibited the most superb and classical galleries of pictures, a large and rare collection of Etruscan vases, precious cameos, medallions, gems, and original drawings of classical authors.

Naples is also decorated with several other beautiful galleries of painting, and cabinets of natural history, belonging to private gentlemen.

The number of colleges or seminaries, public and free schools for the education of youth and children of every description, pious houses for the poor, large, well provided, and commodious hospitals and infirmaries, are as plenty at Naples as in any other capital in the world; and besides this, there are two military colleges, one in the country for the marine, another in the city for the army, with professors of every science belonging to the two branches.

But what is considered quite a privilege of that country, are the two following institutions, viz. three conservatories of music, which, in spite of Mr. Pinkerton, have scattered so many men of distinguished genius in high esteem throughout the world, either to relieve the cares of the human breast, or to afford it additional happiness; and the pious congregation of St. Ivone, made by a subscription of the best counsellors and professors in the law, for the protection of the rights of the poor and indigent. They undertake, gratis, to defend them, and to act in trials and actions in their favour, without any expence whatever. Very often (and it happens mostly in nations of the first rank) the expence of a trial disables the poor people from defending or claiming their own rights, and though born in a free country with a free constitution, yet they may be oppressed by a tyrannic and despotical indigence.

The kingdom of Naples is by no means destitute of a proportioned degree of industry.—Abroad, it has always maintained an active and profitable commerce with France; and at home, Arpino is celebrated for its cloth-manufactories—Taranto for cottons and lana pesce's beautiful work; which is a kind of fine wool taken from a fish, and when dressed and worked, is soft, light, and warm, and more agreeable than silk or cotton, with a colour shining like gold—Vietri for writing and drawing paper; and every where there are a great many soap and silk manufactories. The most celebrated of the latter is at St. Leucio,[1] under the patronage of the

[1] A village near Caserta. The King employed the whole of that population in the silk-manufacture. He took them under his immediate protection, and established for them a particular code of laws, calculated for their peculiar welfare and prosperity. He took care of the education of their children, and by the profit of the manufactory to procure a proper subsistence for their old age, if poor. He regulated and promoted marriages, with a particular kind of ceremony, to be as much as possible congenial and free. In short, it was a very plausible institution, and is one of several instances to prove, that the late Sovereign of Naples

King, where are much admired, not only the quantity and quality of the machinery, but the order and regularity with which the people are kept. It presents an entire population employed in one branch of manufacture, and all kinds of beautiful silk stuffs are worked there. Foreigners visit it with pleasure and admiration: I wish Mr. Pinkerton had seen it. There is also a large iron-manufactory at La Torre dell' Annunziata, which supplies the country with fire and steel arms. In the city of Naples there is a foundry of cannon, and a noble china-manufactory, considered the best in Europe, in point of taste of forms, and miniatures. The application of Etruscan forms to the china-works was originally made there. The King of England possesses a beautiful table-service in that taste, sent to him by his Neapolitan Majesty, as a present, some time ago.

The Court of Naples is luxurious and brilliant; the *delices* or retirements of the Sovereigns are various, magnificent, and open to every person. Caserta *(see note at the end, marked †)* is one of them, very much admired. The country is full of natural wonders and interesting antiquities *(see note marked ‡)*. The climate and

---

was not a tyrant; but he was unfortunately moved by improper advisers to act as such on too many occasions.—Lord Nelson and Sir W. Hamilton, in my opinion, ought to have influenced him better on the late occasion of his return to Naples.

situation are delightful; the people numerous, lively, and hospitable to foreigners, particularly to the English. Public spectacles, academies of music, magnificent theatres, public rooms, and beautiful walks and buildings, greatly abound, with every description of cheap provisions: the common class of people are happy and respectful.

And this is the country where, unluckily, according to his Modern Geography, Mr. Pinkerton could not find any thing deserving notice,[1] excepting priests,[2] despotism, and Giannone; when he could, in honor of truth, have given a more fair account of it, if he had examined the country as a diligent writer ought to have done,

[1] I hope, that any Italian undertaking a similar work of Modern Geography, will, for his own sake, do justice to Great-Britain; for if he should imitate the plan of Mr. Pinkerton, and stop only one day in London, as that gentleman probably did at Naples, and look round the exterior of it with the same degree of prejudice, I am very much afraid he would say, that London is an immense, cold, foggy, damp town, over-run with girls and drunken fellows. All this he might have seen by chance, but every reader would pity him for what he had not seen of England.

[2] Mr. Pinkerton has neglected the *black pigs* of Naples, (which sometimes you meet in some streets,) and that is a great pity. Why not mention them with the over-running priests? They dress in a coat of the same blackness; and if he had united priests, lawyers, and pigs, he would have formed a trio deserving notice.

not only by taking genuine information upon the spot, but examining the objects of curiosity with impartial criticism, and conversing with the best informed people of the nation, as some, but (I am sorry to say) not a great many judicious travellers have done. But Mr. Pinkerton, I fancy, had no time to stop so much in one place, because he had to go round every where, and to speak and decide of every thing under the brilliant title of Modern Geography, which, to be sure, was an immense literary undertaking. But then he must allow me to submit my observations upon what he said rather in a hurry and neglect of the kingdom of Naples. And indeed, if any thing is to be blamed in that portion of Italy, it cannot be for want of study and talents, nor of beauty, comfort, or interest afforded to any impartial observer. I can advance with confidence, that the elocution of the bar, the study of the two sciences, law and music, have always been an exclusive and glorious characteristic of that nation. They could not excel in political elocution, because they had no parliament; nor could they shew their talents in some other branches of learning, being prevented by the restriction of the press, and by national vicissitudes, to which the kingdom of Naples has been at all times subject. But in poetry, literature, history, natural philosophy, physic, and the fine arts, they can boast a Tasso, a Giannone, a Porta, a Baglivi, a Salvator Rosa, a Mazzocchi, and a Bernini, in competition with the Miltons, the Humes, the Newtons, the Sydenhams, and the Reynoldses. As to Mazzocchi and Bernini, it is not in my power to point out in England a learned man, and an architect and sculptor, to be compared with those two Neapolitans. And what would have buried under oblivion any other powerful nation, the ecclesiastical and feudal tyranny, Naples with the spring of its natural genius withstood, and supported with glory its own literary dignity till now, when, I hope, by the removal of these barbarous institutions, a better fate will attend the posterity of that lively nation.

NOTES.

* Page 18.] These four men of honorable memory might have been still alive, to enjoy the love and esteem of their country, if human fallibility had not cut them off during the late political calamities. They were executed in the year 1799, at Naples, when Lord Nelson permitted (if not advised) the well-known infringement of a solemn compact, from the protection of which, they were forced out and condemned as rebels—a melancholy transaction, through which Naples lost the flower of learning and valor. No respect was paid to sex, age, or circumstances. A barbarous junta for more than a year was continually condemning to death, and proscribing upon slight and insufficient charges, immense numbers of deserving citizens. A pregnant lady of rank, called St. Felice, was sentenced to die, because in the time of the Republic, as it was said, she discovered a plot of some ill intentioned individuals, which was to destroy by fire the whole of the city, and by that means produce a counter-revolution. The only kindness bestowed on her was to delay the execution till she was brought to bed. Eleonora Fonseca, a young lady of distinguished talents, shared the same fate, for having written and published the newspaper in the time of the King's absence. Two young lads of noble family, Gensano and Serra, were beheaded, because they had been in the national guard for the protection of public tranquility. The venerable Conforti, when he was executed, was 75 years old. I should distress the reader if I were to go on with this affecting recital of the Neapolitan calamities. It is quite enough to give a slight idea of the incalculable disasters produced by that infamous violation, which could and should have been prevented by Lord Nelson, who had then all the power and influence, and to whom (under a treaty signed by an English representative) the poor injured people in vain applied for justice and redress. They ought to have been sent to France, or to their own home unmolested, according to the stipulated terms; for which purpose a great number of them were already embarked. The writer, as a countryman of those unfortunate victims, submits to English liberality this note of sorrow and complaint, solemnly

NOTES.

protesting, that he rather would have buried in silence the above tragical relation, if he had not considered it as a kind of social duty, to shew to the world that those who are honored with the title of hero, are pleased sometimes to exercise heroism in doing mischief. Who could believe that the Hero of the Nile, the so-called humane Lord Nelson, would have totally lost all sense of justice and humanity at Naples?—*Vide* "Capt. Foote's Vindication, &c." published by Cadell & Davies, 1807; in which the reader will find this curious and very interesting document. He says,—" The idea which the Chief of the Army of the King of Naples entertained of breaking the treaties, may be collected from the conversation which Cardinal Ruffo, (*who was the mentioned Chief of the Army*) Sir William and Lady Hamilton and Lord Nelson, held on board the Foudroyant, as related in Mr. Harrison's Memoirs. The Cardinal maintained, inflexibly, that the treaty ought to be sacred, and upon the following opinion being given in writing by Lord Nelson, the Cardinal retired in disgust."

" Rear-Admiral Lord Nelson, who arrived in the Bay of
' Naples on the 24th of June, with the British fleet, found a
' treaty entered into with rebels, which he is of opinion, ought
' not to be carried into execution without the approbation of
' his Sicilian Majesty."—The Earl of St. Vincent,—Ld. Keith.

How Lord Nelson could entertain for a moment that opinion, is a matter of surprise! since every military person well knows, that capitulations, which are compacts made in the field of battle, are not subject to any ratification—and if with rebels (as his Lordship calls them) terms are inadmissible, that ought to have been taken into consideration before, and not after the stipulation of the treaty. The fact really was, that such a solemn contract, sanctioned by the military agents of the first powers of Europe, as the English, Russians and Turkish were, ought to have been respected in every case. Besides this, Cardinal Ruffo, who entered Naples invested with the same powers as the King himself, and who was called the Vicar of the Kingdom, through the very act of entering into any kind of negociation with rebels, (granting they were such) absolved them from that imputation, at least so far as the validity of the treaty went.

NOTES.

† Page 27.] It is very singular that Mr. Pinkerton's notice should have been so much excited by the "priests and lawyers" at Naples, and not at all by two monuments of grandeur and sublimity at Caserta, only 16 miles from that city: the Great Royal Palace is one, and the Aqueducts are the other. And we see with surprise, that the writer of Modern Geography in describing that part of the world, passes over in perfect silence these two, considered with reason, modern wonders of human ingenuity and power. Perhaps, as they are on so magnificent a scale that no other modern production of that kind in Europe is to be compared with them, he thought that they rather deserved a place among the ancient works, of which he does not professs to speak in his very young and modern treatise. Therefore I must seize this opportunity of giving him the pleasing intelligence, that the very living countrymen of his favorite Neapolitan priests and lawyers, were the genuine constructors of them.

Charles III. of Spain, then King of Naples, in the year 1752, formed the design of them, and the celebrated architect Vanvitelli executed the plan. The palace stands singular in Europe for its size, magnificence, proportion, and riches, which you cannot observe without astonishment. Consider only that the ground occupied by this building, with its dependencies, is the extent of 85 Neapolitan moggi, above 100 English acres of land. Its form is a rectangle, extending from east to west about 731 feet, and from north to south 569, and its height is 106. Three magnificent doors traverse the building through, from the fore to the back part. The interior is divided into four large courts or squares, each of 162 feet by 244. The marble, the number of pillars of one block of beautiful stone which adorn the vestibules, the stairs and the walls some where till 13 feet deep, are of the most surprising elegance and beauty. The height of the palace comprehends five stories, capable of receiving the most numerous court, independent of any extra' building; which advantage makes it superior to the Palace of Versailles, near Paris. There are every sort of accommodation and comfort to supply the wants and luxuries of a large number of

NOTES.

people of every description; even an elegant church and a beautiful theatre. By the back-doors you enter gardens of surprising magnificence, in trees, animals, water, and views. The ground of them is divided into two parts, one flat and extensive next to the palace, the other backwards ascends to a hill, at the top of which there is the famous Belvedere, and a magnificent cascade. These waters were collected from various sources, about 30 Neapolitan miles from Caserta. As the way is interrupted by immense vallies and sharp mountains, the conveyance of the waters was considered very difficult. The ancient Romans, however, had there one of those most conspicuous aqueducts for the transit of what they called Aqua Julia to Capua, perhaps the same waters. It came in the noble mind of King Charles III. to rival them in the construction of an aqueduct superior to their own; and he happily succeeded, for the dimension of the Carolin aqueduct (so called the new one) is rather larger than the ancient.

To level the waters from one mountain to another, the aqueduct forms a bridge, supported by a construction of several rows of arches, one over another, from the bottom to the top of the valley. This work was replied three times, in three different vallies; the elevation of which is considered a master-piece of architecture. The most surprising of these three bridges is the middle one, whose dimensions are 1618 feet of length, and 178 in height; supported by three stories of arches. The first row consists of 19 of them; the second of 27; and the third of 43. La Lande, in describing this bridge, says, that it may contend with every thing of that kind remaining of the ancient Romans: "qui peut (are his words) le disputer à tout ce qui nous est vesté des Romains." Another difficulty arose from the perforation of the mountains, (some being of a very hard stone) through which for several miles the waters were to run. All these works are admirably performed, and the aqueduct, in every point of its construction, represents an object of wonder. Whoever wishes a more satisfactory account of these two curiosities at Caserta, may read the judicious Travels through Italy of Monsieur La Lande, vol. vii. in 8vo.

NOTES.

‡ Page 27.] There is not a spot in the kingdom of Naples which has not a claim to ancient celebrity. History embraces a very remote period of it. Homer, Strabo and Polybius mention the Lestrigones, the Ausones, or the Opices as the most ancient inhabitants of those regions. And according other old writers of the first age of history, all our country from Taranto to Gaeta, and from Lilibeo to Abruzzo Ulterior, before the Trojan war, was divided into small distinct nations. The Phenicians, it is said, to have inhabited a considerable part of the Campania, as they were merchants and adventurers. But never those nations enjoyed a more eminent degree of celebrity than in the time of the Grecian colonies.

After the Trojan war, there happened in Greece, a prodigious emigration, which transformed all our maritime provinces into Grecian colonies. Cumeans, Messenians, Spartans, Eretrians, Cretans, Rodians, Phocians, &c. all denominated heroic nations, came to establish themselves in Sicily and Naples; and by them not only Parthenope, Cuma and Capua were built before the epoch of Rome, but towards that time Siracusa and Catania, and soon after Sibary, Crotone, Locri, Metaponto, Elea, Regio, Possidonia, Siponto, Taranto, Tripergola, Baja, Stabia, Ercolano, Pompei, &c. and they brought with them the degree of culture and civilization that was flourishing in Greece and Egypt. Hence, our Neapolitan provinces proved to be a number of small free estates, governed by wise laws, and in culture and civilization, superior to any other on the continent of Europe. We have from many of those cities, mentioned above, precious monuments of fine arts. Pompei and Herculaneum have filled the Neapolitan museum with classical productions of sculpture and painting. Taranto had in its forum the famous colossal statue of Jupiter, which rivalled that of Rhodes; and the other celebrated colossus of bronze, representing Hercules, which was taken by Fabius Maximus, and carried to the Capitol of Rome. Herodotus, in his sixth book, says, that he saw in the great square of Metaponto the famous statue of Aristea (one of their classical poets) surrounded by laurels; and Ateneus speaks of a laurel-tree of bronze,

NOTES.

dedicated by the Metapontians to Apollo, of a surprising magnitude; and its work was so fine, that in the gentle movement of its delicate leaves by any gust of wind, such an harmonious sound was heard, that the ignorant multitude thought it could both speak and sing.

The monuments of the luxury and magnificence of those ancient provinces are no less numerous. The celebrated Possidonia, now Pestum, is the admiration of the world, for its magnificent ruins. Capua presents to us a beautiful amphitheatre. Pozzuoli, the renowned temple of Jupiter; even the quite destroyed Cuma, has left to us a noble mark of its grandeur, viz. the Arco Felice, an immense arch, the subject of dispute among all the antiquarians about the use of it; and every where you meet with different kinds of ancient works, in aqueducts, temples, baths, and other public buildings. But what has proved more the delicacy of taste, and the high degree in which the fine arts were among our ancient provinces, are the so called Etruscan vases, found in their monuments. It is well known, in what estimation some of them are held, for the quality of the clay, for the taste, elegance, and magnificence of their form, and for the superior merit of the representations in figures around them. Nola has distinguished itself in that sort of vases; for the best vases were found there, and it is supposed, that the Etruscans actually inhabited that country.

But history, besides the evidence of the existing monuments, to prove the flourishing condition of these provinces, has fortunately left to us the memory of a great many distinguished men belonging to them, either as legislators, philosophers, or artists. Pausania, in his sixth book, mentions Patrocles, of Crotone, a famous sculptor, with Learcus, Scillides, and Dipenes, of Reggio. But the most celebrated of them all, was a Pythagoras, who, according to the learned Winckelman, was one of the five best sculptors who flourished after Phydias, in the time of the Pelopponesian war. And we likewise claim as natives of our provinces, the following famous painters: Demophylus of Imera, Silasus of Reggio, and Zeusis of Eraclea. We had an Eraclea near Crotone. See Bayle on the article Zeusis.

NOTES.

As the laws are the support and defence of every civilized country, the ancient Neapolitan provinces produced legislators not inferior in celebrity to the Licurguses, Dracos, and Solons, of the other Greece. Zaleuco, of Locri, was one of them; he established a wise code of laws from the best then collected from Creta, Sparta, and Athens; and from those which he himself created in his country, about 600 years before Christ. Rigorous in the execution of them, he condemned his own son to the punishment of adulterous people, which was, to have the eyes put out; and as an affectionate father, he spared one of them to the son, with the voluntary loss of one of his own.—(Golzius de M. Græcia, page 284.) Timaratus, Saletus, Parmenides, Aristocrates, were all wise legislators of our Grecian provinces; and their repute had been such, that when the Romans resolved to send for an establishment of laws from the wisdom of Greece, it is the opinion of many antiquarians, that they did send to our provinces for the laws of the twelve tables, and not to the other Greece.

Pythagoras, the famous ancient philosopher, came to inhabit Crotone after his long travels through Egypt, Greece, Persia, and India. It was towards the year 546 before Christ, that he came to establish himself in Italy. It is said, that such was the power of his elocution, that by his first speech he made to the Crotonians, he obtained 2000 followers.—(Giamblicus Life of Pythagoras.) He taught philosophy for a very long time in Crotone and Metaponto, and married a woman of the former town, by whom he had a large family. His science was spread in our provinces, and served to improve their culture, while all the continent of Europe was still barbarous. He was great not only in physic, but in metaphysics, astronomy, mathematics, and morality; in every one of which sciences he was a discoverer or the founder of a system. It is astonishing what progress his doctrine made through the world, and we may say with confidence, that to this great philosopher any other afterwards is indebted, for the principle and solidity of subsequent discoveries or improvements in sciences and morality.

We reckon three sects of Pythagoreans: one was called the Jonian, spread throughout old Greece, and particularly in the

NOTES.

Jonian province. The other two were the Italian and the Aleatica, both belonging to our Italian provinces, and the remaining of Italy. The antiquarian Fabricius, in his Bibliotheca Græca, lib. xi. attempts to give a number of the most celebrated Pythagoreans of Italy, and he reaches the number of 200, of which 13 were Sicilians, and the remainder were all of our Magna Greece, viz. 34 of Crotone, 42 of Metaponto, 41 of Taranto, 15 of Locri, 9 of Lucania, 10 of Reggio, 11 of Sibary, 2 of Turo, 4 of Possidonia, and 2 of Elea. The most celebrated of Crotone was Telauge, the very son of Pythagoras; who left a book, entitled de Tetrade, which was given by him on his death-bed to his daughter Damo, with the command not to publish or give it to any body. After her death, however, it fell in the hands of Philolao, another Pythagorean of Crotone, who sold it to Plato for the price of 400 mines, about 100 pounds. And with the help of this very book, it is said, Plato composed his own of The World. Menon, Aristens, Milo, Alcmeon, (who was the first dissector and anatomist,) were all of Crotone.

Leo was the most celebrated of Metaponto, he is considered the author of the Elements of Geometry.

Among many distinguished Pythagoreans of Taranto, Archytas enjoyed the first reputation. He was the ruler of his country, not only by his political wisdom, but by his celebrity in the sciences, both of mathematics and mechanics. He was the discoverer of flying bodies. His flying wooden dove, mentioned by Aulo Gellio, lib. x. c. 12, is not unknown to the world. And from him originated the Dedalian science in Italy, which has been revived lately among us. To him we are indebted for a great many useful discoveries, which may be seen in the Bibliotheca Græca of Fabricius, and from the antiquarians Mantucla and Brukerus. Of this great man, Horace speaks with enthusiasm, in his eleventh book, ode xxviii.

Taranto produced three other illustrious Pythagoreans, viz. Archippus, Lysis, and Aristoxenes. The first had the honor of the foundation of the famous school at Thebes. The second was the preceptor of Epaminondas; and the

NOTES.

third was a great musician, from whom we derive three books on the Elements of Harmony.

Timeus, of Locri, was great in astronomy and natural philosophy: his famous book, De Natura Mundi, was likewise the guide of Plato in his dialogue entitled Timeus. Cicero gives an account of him in his work, De Finibus.

Aresa, of Lucania, directed the Pythagorean school; and Ocellus, of the same country, composed the celebrated book, De Universo. He supposes the world, as to its matter and form, to be eternal.

Finally, for the sake of brevity, I shall conclude with Parmenides and Zenon, of Elea or Velia, a town near Poestum, the two famous institutors of the Pythagorean sect called Eleatica. Parmenides is considered the most learned of antiquity in physic and astronomy. All that he said of the universe without the help of instruments, has been verified by modern philosophers. His opinion was, that the universe is composed of suns and moons, and that our moon is enlightened by the sun—that she has a very unequal superfice, being full of mountains, plains, and seas—and is inhabited the same as our own earth. He discovered the Esperus and Phosphorus to be the same planet, Venus—that the universe was what we may call God, one, immense, eternal, invariable. In short, he described the true philosophy of heavens, as received in our present times. It is a pity that there are no books extant of this great man's, for it is said, upon the authority of Plato, that he composed a great many works in prose, and a course of philosophy in verse.

Zeno succeeded Parmenides. This surprising philosopher was the inventor of the art of reasoning, called Dialectica. It is said, that no body could answer the power of his arguments; and according to Bayle, in the article Zeno, Aristotle did himself little honor in answering Zeno's objections against the movement. He had a kind of argument called sorite, of which he made use in the support of his doctrine; but he went so far as to pretend to prove, that there was nothing in the world--perhaps for the purpose of shewing his power of argument only.

NOTES.

This famous Pythagorean school, however, which did so much honor to the Neapolitan Magna Græcia, and to the human understanding in general, did not last more than 200 years after the arrival of Pythagoras at Crotone. The prevailing party of the Aristocrats of Magna Græcia is supposed to have contributed to the destruction of the Pythagorean college, which by a popular insurrection was burnt to ashes. And Polybius says, in his books 11 and 12, that all our provinces were then distracted by dreadful seditions. So, little by little the Pythagoreans disappeared, and another philosophical school took place, which was that of Socrates. Hence, the Academicians, the Peripateticians, and Stoicians. And our provinces shared in the glory of these new doctrines, by producing many of distinguished talents, as Timaratus, Clinomacus, Hippones of Reggio, and Strasea of Naples.

The political independence of Magna Græcia diminished when she was conquered by the Romans. The policy of these conquerors was to make themselves great upon the humiliation of those countries which they over-run. But the natural genius of the people, no longer of Greek but semi-Greek provinces, never ceased to give marks of glory and distinction in every branch of learning, as we have successively demonmonstrated in the foregoing pages. And when the Barbarians came to desolate the whole of Italy, and the darkness of ignorance was spread all over the face of Europe, we, the Neapolitans professed still wisdom and literature. Not only of the great Cassiodoro, mentioned in this tract, who lived about the fifth century of our æra, but we have memoirs of distinguished men in the worst times of barbarism.— John Diaconus, of the Neapolitan cathedral, lived in the tenth century. He was learned in the Greek and Latin languages, and wrote the Chronicle of the Neapolitan Bishops. Another, Peter Subdiaconus, prosecuted the same Chronicle till the year 880. Erchemberto, of Benevento, wrote the history of Longobards. And the celebrated monastery of Montecasino kept learning alive as much as the barbarism of those times would permit.

NOTES.

§ Page 28.] If the reader be an Englishman, he will smile perhaps, at my assertion that the lower class of Neapolitans are happy. A strong prejudice seems to prevail in England, which makes the people think, that we abroad are all slaves and unhappy wretches, groaning under depotism; this has been boldly and very often advanced before me in companies. On which account, I beg leave to submit the following observations. It is true, that the Neapolitan people do not enjoy the privilege of electing Members of Parliament, and of being treated in public-houses during the election, by the rich canditate, for the sake of their vote. They do not enjoy the liberty of abusing, hissing, and even stoning a member of the opposite party, nor the pleasure of carrying him, whom they have elected, on their own shoulders. But then they enjoy other advantages, which might be considered as an ample compensation or balance; for instance, they have no coal-mines to work, no impress to endure; they never enter for life under military service, nor is even the name of the frightful Income-Tax known to them. The mode of supporting their existence is easy: provisions are both abundant and cheap; and especially vegetables, fruits, Indian corn, chesnuts, are procured for almost nothing. Under a clear sky they require fewer necessaries of life, and enjoy more hours of leisure; and it is not necessary for some of them even to work all the days of the week. Hence originate their lively and happy looks.

It is equally true, that the plan of the English Constitution is admirable for the protection of freedom, and for the balance of political powers; but the execution of it with purity, that is to say, free from abuses and corruption, seems to have been always a matter of the most difficult nature; at least, as difficult as ever in more absolute governments, was, the happy chance of a wise, virtuous, and magnanimous monarch.— And in case these two rarities should happen, I declare, with the opinion of the best politicians, that the government of a philosophic Prince intrusted with supreme authority, is by far preferable. And when both are corrupt, I cannot tell which of the two despotisms is to be considered the worst.

NOTES.

Then the English constitution becomes an oligarghical monster, covered with the sacred veil of freedom.

Let us not be deceived: history, which is called the light of truth and the rule and mistress of human life, has no other periods of happiness to shew, as Gibbon wisely observes, than those under " Vespasian, Titus, Nerva, Trajan, Adrian, Antoninus Pius, and Marcus Aurelius, all good princes and philosophers;" nor any more glorious, or in which united to martial laurels flourished so much talent in arts and sciences, than those of Pericles, or Alexander the Great, Augustus, Medicis, and Louis XIV. I want then to learn from the annals of mixed or free governments, if any epoch thereof was ever considered of the same magnitude. Alfred, Charlemagne, Francis I., Henry IV., Peter the Great, not to mention many others in ancient and modern records, such as Numa, Cyrus, and Napoleon, contributed with their wisdom in the narrow compass of their life, to the improvement and glory of their own people, more than any free constitution ever did in more extended periods.

Evans, Printer, Bristol.

Printed by Libri Plureos GmbH in Hamburg, Germany